Monographic Journals of the Near East *Assur* 2/2 (September 1979)

HURRIAN PERSONAL NAMES IN THE RIMAH ARCHIVES

Jack M. Sasson
University of North Carolina

This study collects, under section II, the Hurrian personal names preserved in the Old Babylonian tablets uncovered at Tell al-Rimah. A smaller list (II,1) gives names which cannot be analyzed by the author. The third section (III) presents a list of Hurrian elements involved in making up the names. While it is stressed that names of Hurrian coinage do not necessarily reflect Hurrian ethnicity, an introduction: 1. gives statistics on the names of Hurrian derivation; 2. discusses the stratification of Hurrians within Rimah's society and 3. speaks to the 'ethnic' concentration of Hurrians during the various phases of Old Babylonian Rimah.

Contents

I. Introduction

In introducing the "Iltani archive" and the "Temple Texts," Stephany Dalley devoted a paragraph to summarizing her analysis of the ethnic distribution of personal names extracted from 243 Old Babylonian documents from al-Rimah (Karana):[1]

> An analysis of the linguistic groups to which the personal names in the Iltani archives and temple texts...belong was undertaken in detail in my thesis. A very few minor alterations have been made, and the results only are given here...

[1] Stephany Dalley, C. B. F. Walker, and J. D. Hawkins, *The Old Babylonian Tablets from Tell al Rimah*. British School of Archaeology in Iraq, 1976, p. 38.

	Total no.	Akk.%	Amor.%	Hurr.%
Iltani archive	177	35.0	26.5	15.8
Temple texts	96	9.4	7.3	42.7

While preparing a review of the Rimah volume I found it advisable to develop my own analysis of this documentation, both because Dalley's own complete analysis remains unpublished, available only to those with access to her 1970 dissertation submitted to the School of Oriental and African Studies, University of London, and because the OB documentation from al-Rimah consists now of over 100 additional texts and seal inscriptions.

The following essay, concentrating on the Hurrian personal names from al-Rimah, joins others which attempt to gauge the Hurrian presence in the Mesopotamian Middle Euphrates-Tigris valleys.[2] I will readily admit that often such surveys of the personal names do not reduce this decades-old discussion.[3] At the least, however, they do provide us with a larger corpus of Hurrian personal names from the Middle Bronze age, while, at the same time supplementing the lexical and grammatical data of a language not precisely understood as yet.

This account closely follows my earlier effort which assessed Mari's Hurrian onomasticon.[4] That assessment was criticized for its content by Edzard[5] and praised for its format and aim by J.-M. Durand.[6] It will be noticed that my selection of Rimah names for inclusion in the study will not be guided by overly rigid criteria. Once names of Semitic, Sumerian, and Elamite coinage were extracted from the Rimah corpus, the remainder have been subjected to analysis for possible Hurrian makeup. Thirty percent of these names (about 140 examples) were found to be "certifiably" Hurrian. The 36 examples (twenty percent) which were questionable I nevertheless retained under analysis, but was careful to follow each entry by an [H?] to indicate my uneasiness concerning their analysis. Those names which have not yielded to my analysis are listed below, *sub.* II.1.

One feature of my Mari treatment in *UF* will not be duplicated here. There will not be a listing of towns and villages, outside of Rimah/Karana itself, with which persons bearing names of Hurrian derivations were associated.[7] In the Mari article I took the opportunity to give a profile of the ethnic make-up of localities which included persons of Hurrian appellation. Since many of these places played a major role in the history of the Upper and Middle Euphrates, there were benefits to be drawn from such an exercise. The same is hardly the case when it comes to the towns and villages that are listed in the Rimah archives. With the possible exception of Qaṭara (8 PNs), none of the localities with which Hurrian-named individuals were associated seem to have been more than provincial hamlets [Ašala (1 PN); Badrum (2 PNs); Bununewa (1 PN); Ḫamadanum (1 PN); Ḫurnat (1 PN); Kašpanim (2 PNs); Marata (6 PNs); Marikatum (1 PN); Meš[xx] (1 PN); Rataman (5 PNs); Ṣilliya (1 PN); Turḫam [unclear reading of the GN] (1 PN); Zabri (4 PNs); Zari[xx] (2 PNs); [x]zabirima (1 PN)]. It should be

2 Alalaḫ: A. Draffkorn [-Kilmer]: *Hurrians and Hurrian at Alalaḫ: An Ethnolinguistic Analysis.* (Doctoral Dissertation, University of Pennsylvania, 1959); Mari: J. M. Sasson, "Hurrians and Hurrian Names in the Mari Texts," *Ugarit-Forschungen*, 6 (1974), 353-400; *Dilbat:* D. Charpin, "L'Onomastique Hurrite à Dilbat et ses implications historiques," *Problèmes concernant les Hurrites* [Centre National de la Recherche Scientifique: Centre de Recherches Archéologiques. Méthodologie et Critiques, 1 (Publication de l'U.R.A., 8. Mémoires)]. Paris, 1977, 51-70. Still to be assessed are the personal names of Hurrian coinage in the Chagar-Bazar texts.

3 J.-M. Durand's somewhat tendentious *mis-au-point* could be recommended as a recent statement on the problems, "L'Insertion des Hurrites dans l'histoire proche-orientale: problematique et perspectives," in *Problèmes concernant les Hurrites*, 21-40.

4 J. M. Sasson, *UF* 6(1974), 353-400.

5 *RLA*, IV, 510b: "wohl zu weit gehende Einbeziehung von Namen."

6 Durand, *Problèmes . . . Hurrites*, 39, n.26.

7 Sasson, *UF* 6(1974), 390-393.

noted, however, that Badrum, Bununewa, and Ḫurnat may have contained provincial palaces, at least during the reign of Ḫaqba-Ḫammu.

Statistics on the percentage of Hurrian-based personal names cannot really tell us much on the ethnic makeup of a particular city-state. First, because it is extremely difficult to attach a large number of personal names to a specific locality. Since names of Hurrian derivation may have been borne by foreign persons, whose presence in the Rimah area was accidental, their inclusion in any statistical survey could only distort proposed conclusions. Furthermore, it would be imprudent to assume that a name with Hurrian etymology necessarily reflects Hurrian ethnicity. This point could be substantiated by turning to the results obtained by Charpin and, to a lesser degree, by me.[8] It is unfortunate that both at Rimah and at Mari scribes and bureaucrats did not find it necessary to record patronymics. The one case in which two generations of names were preserved at Rimah indicates that, while the father bore an apparently Hurrian name (Zili-pan), the son had an Akkadian name (Bēlī-ašarid).

The data derived from the listing of Hurrian personal names given below, however, do allow us to make the following assertions and observations:

1. Statistics of Persons with Names of Hurrian Coinage

	A	B	C	?
Total PNs (176)	125	3	46	2
Total Males (155)	123	3	28	2
Total Females (21)	2	0	18	1
males [H?] (31)	28	0	3	1
females [H?] (5)	4	0	1	0
total * (44)	34	0	10	0

Explanation of symbols

[H?] = Hurrian derivation of names uncertain
* = names associated with persons who lived in villages and towns outside Rimah/Karana (?)
(A) = (early) Šamši-Adad historical period
(B) = Ḫatnu-rapi historical period
(C) = Iltani/Ḫaqba-Ḫammu historical period

2. Social Stratification

Hurrian-named individuals do not seem to belong to any specific stratum of society.

2.1 During period (A)

Our data is composed overwhelmingly of male names. While most of these names are borne by persons whose functions are not delineated, we could note the presence of one tax official, seven middle-echelon bureaucrats, and one e n g a r. We note that text 276, of unclear dating because it was found in loose fill, is a docket which contains the single name of a Hurrian woman.

2.2. During periods (B) and (C).

The evidence from this period is much more variegated and instructive. No doubt this is so because it is partially derived from epistolary documents. Most surprising is the fact that three *limu* names (and especially the second and third) *could* be analyzed as Hurrian: Atta, Attara, and Tuttaya. In addition to a

8 On these two points, see Charpin, *Problèmes . . . Hurrites*, 63-64 [2.3.2.1--2.3.2.3]; Sasson, *UF* 6 (1974), 355.

number of menial workers, both males and females [fem. weavers (5 PNs); fem. servants (11 PNs); fullers (1 of each sex)], the listings include a fisherman, a wine supervisor, a kitchen head (fem.); a wool controller, a physician, a number of middle-rank officials (five male, one female), and a king's companion.

3. 'Ethnic' Concentration

A number of texts from Periods (A) and (C) consist of listings which record a large percentage of names of persons with Hurrian appellative.

3.1. During period (A)

Text 225 contains 9 names associated with the hamlet of Zabri; at least 4 of these names are Hurrian in coinage. Of the 25 names that are still complete in text 224, only 4 could be attributed to Semitic coinage; of the rest two are unclear and the remainder has been analyzed below. Text 227 contains two names both of which are analyzed below as possibly Hurrian. Three of the 7 complete names in text 230 can be attributed to Hurrian coinage. Texts 231 and 233 contain a large percentage of names of Hurrian origin. There is no hint as to the function or purpose of the above mentioned texts. Text 322 impresses by the large number of Hurrian-named individuals associated with Qaṭara.

3.2. During Period (C)

Text 146 is written to Iltani by the Hurrian-named correspondent Šawalum-nadki. Dalley suggests that the latter (sex uncertain) was a relative of Ḫaqba-Ḫammu (p. 120). Since Šawalum-nadki's messenger also bears a Hurrian appellative, it may be that the milieu whence this text originated included a healthy number of Hurrians.

Text 188 records the outlay of barley to two persons with Hurrian names.

Finally, we note that text 206 and its duplicating variants 207-209 contain a great number of names of Hurrian coinage. Those recorded within were menial workers, both male and female, who likely worked in Rimah's palace.[9]

II. List of Names

Agap-šeni

(A) *a-ga-ap-še-ni* 322:vi:1!

Akata-tupki

(A) *a-ka-ta-tu-up-ki* 224:20

Aku-luk [H?]

(C) *a-ku-lu-uk* 81:8 LÚ.TÚG

Allaš-arum

(A) *al-la-aš-a-rum* 229:5; 236:2; 238:2; 321:vii:4'; 322:i:29'

Alpu-adal

(A) *al-pu-a-dal* 317:18

fAlpuš-allai

(?) f*al-pu-úš-al-la-i* 276. Name on docket

[9] E. Cassin and J.-J. Glassner's *Anthroponomie et Anthropologie de Nuzie, Volume 1: Les Anthroponymes*, Undena Publications, 1977, reached me after this paper was accepted for publication. I have therefore made minimal use of its contents. It will be cited as *AAN*.

Alpu-ya — (A) *al-pu-ya* 244:ii:50; 321:ii:9 From *tu*[*x*]^{ki}

fAlu(m)-naya — (C) *a-lu-na-ya* 206:ob.:2; 209:4 } weaver.
a-lu-um-na-⌈*ya*⌉ 207:ii:2; (cf. 208:ii:2) } weaver.

Aman-taḫi (M) — (C) *a-ma'-an'-ta-ḫi* 318:18. Tax official.

Aniš-kipal (M) — (?) *a-ni-iš-ki-ba-al* 277:2. (discussion of the royal name in UF 6(1974), 358)

Aran-[xx] — (A) *a-ra-an-*[*xx*] 229:13.

Ari-[xx] — (A) **a-ri-i-*[*xx*] 248:6'. From Kašpanim.

Ari-ya(pa?) — (A) **a-ri-ya* 232:10. I would prefer to read this name *a-ri-ya-pa*, taking the last sign as *-pa* rather than Dalley's UGULA. From Marata.

Arip-Teššub (M) — (A) *a-ri-ip-te-eš-šu-ub* 224:12; 229:[9]

Arum-adal — (A) *a-ru-um-a-dal* 224:26. Cf. Mari's *Arim-adal*.

Arum-mušni — (B) *a-rum-mu-úš-ni* 18:8. Official.

Atta [H?] — (C) *a-at-ta* 263:9. *limu*-name

fAttap-naya — (C) *f*at-ta-ap?-na-a-ya* 144:16. Lives in fAzzu's hometown.

Atta-ra [H?] — (C) *a-at-ta-ra* 215:10. *limu*-name.

Awi-ziri — (A) *a-wi-zi-ri* 239:2. Pays taxes.

Awi-yazu — (A) *a-wi-ya-zu* 244:ii:28'. Cf. Mari's Awi-yazi

Azip-nan — (A) *a-zi-ip-na-an* 318:6. Official.

fAzzen — (A) *faz-ze-en* 323:3

fAzzu (M) — (C) **faz-zu* 143:3
**a-az-zu-ú* 144:2; *fa-az-zu-ú* 188:3; 202:7; 203:10 (Important official, corresponds with Iltani on an equal level. Unknown hometown)

fAzzu-e (M) — (C) *az-zu-e* 207:i:10; 208:i:10

⸢Azzu-ena

1?. (C) *⸢*az-zu-e-na* 160:3 LÚ [*sic*] *a-ša-la-yi-tum*⸣. (daughter (?) of Mutu-ḫadki). Same as Azzu (?)
2?. (C) **az-zu-e-na* 153:6. Lives in Andariq (?).
3?. (C) *az-zu-e-na* 207:i:[14]; 208:i:14. Palace servant.

Eḫli-a[xx]

(C) *eḫ-li-a*[-*xx*] 267:19. His LÚ GÌR. SIG$_5$.GA received grain.

Eḫli-ya

(A) *eḫ-li-ya* 229:10

Ella-[xx] [H?]

(A) *e-el-la*[-xx] 279:10

Ella-li

(A) *el-la-li* 321:ii:8

Elli

(A) **el-li 228:3. A sāmiḫum*, 'wine- presser', at Badrum

Era-ti [H?]

(A) *e-ra-ti* 231:4. Listed in a text in which Hurrian PN predominates

Ḫalu-li [H?]

(A) *ḫa-lu-li*? 324:7. Temple personnel.

Ḫamma-ta [H?]

(A) *ḫa-am-ma-ta* 318:11. Minor official.

Ḫapi-ya [H?] (M)

(A) *ḫa-bi-ya* 244:iii:24'

Ḫaši-ya

(A) **ḫa-ši-ya* 232:3. From Marata.

Hazip-aranzi (M)

1. (A) *ḫa-zi-ip-a* ⸢*-ra-an-zi*⸣ 231:15
2?. (C) **ḫa-zi-ip* ⸢*a-ra-*⸣*an-zi* 257:7 Official in (?) Buninewa

Ḫazip-mu[xx]

(A) *ḫa-zi-ip-mu*[-xx] 322:v:36

Ḫazip-Šimiga

1. (A) **ḫa-zi-ip-ši-mi-ga* 231:18; 322:ii:14' (from Qaṭara).
2?. (C) *ḫa*⸢*-zi-ip-*⸣*ši-mi-ga* 218:4. Official, in charge of meat dispensations?

Ḫazi-ya

1. (A) **ḫa-zi*[*-ya*?] 244:ii:23'. From Rataman.
2?. (A) **ḫa-zi-ya* 228:2. A *sāmiḫum* from Badrum.

Ḫirši-tta

(A) *Ḫi-ir-ši-it-ta* 224:19; 230:6'

Ḫirzi-ya

1-2. (A) *ḫi-ir-zi-ya* 322:iv:22; v:23, 32

Ḫiu-ya [H?]

(A) *ḫi-ú-ya* 224:31. In a text in which Hurrians predominate

Ḫu-ena

1. (A) **ḫu-e-*⸢*na*⸣ 322:i:42'. From Qaṭara.
2. (A) **ḫu-*⸢*e*⸣*-na* 322:v:25. From [xx]rum.

Irip-zi [H?]

(A) *i-ri-ip-si* 233:5 *(ša mi-a-ti)*

Irri-ki

(A) *ir-ri-gi* 233:6. ENGAR?

Itḫen-adal

(A) **it-ḫe-en-a-dal* 322:i:36'. From Qaṭara.

Itḫiya

(A) *it-ḫi-ya* 321:i:2

Izza-zzi

(A) **iz-za-az-zi* 322:ii:12'. From Qaṭara.

Kaba-nnu [H?]

(A) *ka-ba-an-nu* 326:10

Kabi-nni

(A) *ka-bi-in-ni* 321:i:10

Kabi-ya (M)

(A) **ka-bi-i-ya* 248:ob. 2. From Kaspanim.

Kakki-še

(A) *ka-ak-ki-še* 231:9

Kak-zu [H?]

(A) *ka-ak-su* 322:vi:31!

Kanaku-urši [H?]

(A) **ka-na-ku-ur-ši* 225:7. From Zabri.

Kani-[xx] [H?]

(A) *ka-ni-[xx]* 244:ii:53'

Kani-azzu

(C) **ka-ni-az-zu* 146:9, 12. Messenger to Iltani.

Kani-ya

1. (A) **ka-ni-ya* 308:6. Receives land in Marikatum.
2?. (A) **ka-ni-ya* 322:i:11'. From Qaṭara.

Kan(n)a-ya

1. (A) *ka-na-a-ya* 230:7'
2?. (A) **ka-an-na-a-ya* 232:6. From Marata.

Kanza-azni [H?]
(uncertain division)

(A) *ka-an-za-az'-ni'* 224:11

Kanza-ni

(A) **ka-an-za-ni* 322:i:17'. From Qaṭara.

Kap-tupki

(A) **ga-ap-tu-up-ki* 322:iii:12'. From Zari[xx]

Katir-ḫi (M)

(A) *ka-ti-ir-ḫi* 224:25; 322:vi:35

Ken-kiya/ziya

(A) *ki-en-gi/zi-ya* 321:vii:6'. Cf. *ki-en-zi-ya*, below.

Kenzu-kate [H?]

(A) *ki-en-zu-ga-te* 323:5

Kinni-ya [H?]

(C) **ki-in-ni-ya* 253:8. Wine supervisor in Ḫurnat (?).

Kinzi-ya

(A) *ki-in-zi-ya* 244:ii:45'. Cf. Ken-kiya, above

Kizzi

1. (A) *ki'-iz-zi* 289:4
2?. (C) *ki-iz-zi* 206:rev:8; 207:iii:7; 208:iii:7; 211:9. Fuller

Kizzi-pa [H?]

(A) *ki-iz-zi-ba* 322:v:26

Kizzi-pu [H?]

(A) *ki-iz-zi-bu* 244:iii:26'

Kui-tanu [H?]

(C) *ku-i-ta-nu* 217:2. Controls wool.

Kullu [H?]

(A) *ku-ul-lu* 227:2

^{f}Kul-zipaya

Perhaps divide into Kulzi-paya

(C) *ku-ul-zi-pa-a-*⌜*ya*⌝ 207:i:9 } Palace servant
ku-ul-zi-pa-ya 208:i:9

Kun-tanu

(A) *ku-un-ta-nu* 224:5. Listed among Hurrian PNs.

Kunu-zaḫi

(A) *ku-nu-za-ḫi* 322:i:19'

Kupa-ta [H?]

1. (A) *ku-ba-ta* 321:i:3
2?. *ku-ba-ta* 321:vii:2'

^{f}Kuta-ti (M)

(C) *ku-da-di* 207:i:4; 208:i:⌜4⌝. Palace servant.

Kuti-ya

(A) *ku-ti-ya* 322:iv:20

Kutu-kka

(A) *ku-tu-uk-*⌜*ka*⌝ 229:11

Kuzi-zu

(A) *ku-zi-zu* 321:vi:⌜3'⌝; 322:i:16'

^{f}Menna (M)

(C) ^{f}*me-en-na* 171:4; 190:⌜3⌝. Receives grain.
me-en-na 207:i:6; 208:i:6. Palace servant;210:5 (MÍ *ša be-el-ti*)

$^{(f)}$Menen-kaššil [H?]

(C) *me-ni-e-en-ka-aš-ši-il* 206:rev:13
⌜*me*⌝*-ni-in-ka-aš-ši-il* 207:iii:17. Among MÍ^{MEŠ} *ša* É ^{f}*il-ta-ni*.

Mennu-laya

(C) *me-en-nu-la-ya* 207:i:19; *me-en-nu-la-a-ya* 208:i:19. Young palace servant.

Muzun-adal

(A) *mu-zu-un-a-dal* 244:ii:13'. Cf. Mari's Muzan-adal

^{f}Nalu-kadil [H?]

(C) *na-lu-ka-di-il* 210:10 MÍ *ša be-el-ti*

Nan-adal

(A) *na-an-na-dal* 231:11

Nawa-nu [H?]

(A) *na-wa-nu* 244:11:51'

Nawar-adal (M)

(A) *na-wa-ar-a-dal* 317:21

Nunna-kka

(A) *nu-un-na-ak-ka* 224:27

Nupur-šarri

(C) *nu-pur-šar-ri* 252:⌜6⌝; 261:10; Seal ⌜#6.⌝ Official who eats at the king's table. (Note Mari's Nupar-šarri.)

Nu-ya

(A) *nu-ú-ya* 224:32

Nuza-ma

(A) *nu-za-ma* 321:ii:20

Paki-ya

(A) **pa-gi-ya* 246:6'. From [x]zabirima

Pala-tanu [H?]

(A) *ba-la-ta-nu* 322:ii:20'

Papa-zzu [H?]

(A) **ba-ba-az-zu* 246?:4. From Meš-[x].

Pap(p)i-zu [H?]

(C) *pa-ap-pí-su* 206:rev:7; 207:iii:6 208:iii:6; 209:26' } Fuller
pa-pí-su 211:8.

Pazzi-ku [H?]

(A) ⌜*ba*⌝-*az*-⌜*zi*⌝-*ku* 224:38

Peza-nu [H?]

(A) **be-za-nu* 244:ii:18'. From Rataman.

fPuzum-ki

(C) *pu-zu-um-gi* 206:obv:8'; 207:ii:8; 208:ii:8; 209:10'. Weaver.

Šaduk-adal

(C) **ša-du-uk-a-dal* 252:4; 256:rev: 5. Receives an allotment of wine when he visits at Buninewa.

Šaḫeš-adal

(A) *ša-ḫi-eš-a*-⌜*dal*⌝ 321:i:12

fŠalan-zar

1. (C) *ša-la-an-za-ar* 206:obv :3; 207:ii:3; 208:ii:[3]; 209:5'; 211:1. Weaver.
2. (C) *ša-la-an-za-ar* 206:Obv:15; 207:ii:15; 208:ii:15 [MÍN]; 209:17'; 211:4. Weaver.

Šama-ḫul(i) (M)

(A) *ša-ma-ḫu-li* 238:4. Pays *šibšum* taxes.
ša-ma-ḫu'- ul/li 322:i:28'. Very likely the same man because of other PNs shared in 238 and 322.

Šattum-ar[xx]

(A) **ša-at-tum-ar-*[*xx*] 322:ii:16. From Qaṭara.

Šawalum-nadki

(C) **ṣa*-PI-*lum-na-ad-ki* 146:3. Writes to Iltani. her/his É$^{!}$GI$_4$ (= *kallatum* ?). Dispatches a Hurrian messenger, Kani-azzu.

^{f}Šeḫlum-tari

(C) *še-eḫ-lum-ta-ri* 206:obv:⌜6⌝; 207:ii:6; 208:ii:⌜6⌝; 209:8'. Weaver.

^{f}Šeke-šše [H?]

(C) *še-ge-eš-še* 207:i:13; 208:i:13. Palace servant.

Šennip-anu [H?]

(A) **še-in-ni-ba-nu* 247:obv:6' [name may be preceded by one more sign]. From Hamadanim.

Šešwe

(A) *še-eš*-PI 233:2 [If not for another citation of the name, this PN may be read *še-eš*-PI-*na$^{!}$-ya$^{!}$*]. Tax involvements.
318:8. Subsection chief. Collects taxes?

Šikku-z(z)i

(A) *ši-ik-ku-uz-zi* 300:7
ši-ik-ku-zi 278:5,17 } Lower echelon official.

^{f}Šila-llu

(A) ^{f}*ši-la-al-lu* 183:5 ; 184:5; 185:4. heads kitchen. Dalley divides into (Semitic?) Ši-lallu (for Ši-lalû?).

Šuku-pi [H?]

(A) **šu-ku-bi* 322:v:33. From [xx]rum.

Šur-e (M)

(A) *šu-re-e* 244:iii:14'$^{!}$

Taḫi (M)

(A) **ta-ḫi* 224:24; 225:9. From [Z]abri.

Taki-[xx] [H?]

(A) *ta-ki-*[*xx*] 321:ii:3.

Taki-ya (M)

(A) *ta-ki-ya* 321:ii:7

Tallu-ḫul

(A) *ta-al-lu-*⌜*ḫu-ul*⌝ 236:6; 224:28 (*ta-al$^{!}$-lu$^{!}$-ḫu-ul*)

Talpu-nu-PI-ri/
(or)
Talpunu-wari/ewri

(A) *ta-al-pu-nu*-PI-*ri* 224:33 (read perhaps *ta-al-mu$^{!}$*. .)

Tampu-nunu [H?]

(A) *ta-am-bu-nu-nu* 224:16

Tata-kka

(A) *ta-da-ak-ka* 318:19. Head of a section.

^{f}Tati-enna

(C) *ta-di-en-na* 206:obv:13; 207:ii:13; 208:ii:13; 209:15'; 211:5. Weaver.

^{f}Tazu-laya

(C) *ta-su-la-ya* 211:3. 206:obv:12; 209:14' [MÍ.TUR]; 207:ii:12; 208:ii:[12] [TUR]. Weaver.

Teš(š)sub-ewri
(A) *te-eš-šu-ub*-PI-*ri* 224:23; 231:6
2?. *⌜te⌝-šu-ub*-PI-*ri* 322:iii:17'. From Zari[xx].

Tiri-kka
(A) *ti-ri-ik-ka* 231:7

ᶠTizi-ḫam (M)
(C) *ti-zi-ḫa-am* 206:rev:4; 207:iii:3; 208:iii:3; 209:23'; 211:6 [MÍ]. Fuller. (In Mari, a male name).

Tukki-[xx]
(A) **tu-uk-ki-*[*xx*] 322:i:39'. From Qaṭara.

Tulpi-ya
(A) **tu-ul-pí-ya* 244:ii:16' [From Rataman]. 246:6 [from [xx]].

Tupki-[xx]
(A) **tu-up-ki-*[*xx*] 244:i:8'. From Ṣilliya.

Tupki-ya
(C) *tu-up-ki-ya* 58:15. Physician [*asû*]

Tutta-ya [H?]
(A) *tu-ut-ta-ya* 315:6. *Limu*-name

ᵈU.GUR-adal (M)
(C) ᵈU.GUR-a-dal 186:4. Receives barley.

ᶠUke
(C) *ú-ge* 207:i:11;⌜208:i:11⌝. Palace servant. 210:6 [MÍ *ša be-el-ti*]

Ukka-[ya?]
(A) **uk-ka-*[*ya?*] 232:4. From Marata.

Uku-nnu
(A) *ú-ku-un-nu* 244:iii:25'.

⁽ᶠ⁾Unap-eli
(C) *ú–na-ap-e-li* [207:i:16] [TUR]; 208:i:16. Palace servant.

Unap-še (M)
(A) *ú-na-ap-še* 317:1. Receives land.
[Division uncertain, perhaps Unuš-(š)e or even Unuš-e]

Unu-še
(A) *ú-nu-še* 224:34

Ura-ni
(A) **ú-ra-ni* 225:8 From [Za]bri. Note Mari's *ú-ra-nu*, XVIII:62:10

ᶠUte-na [H?]
(C) *ú-te-na* 207:i:18; 208:i:18 [TUR]. Palace servant. Cf. Mari's *ú-di-na*.

Utu-ḫu [H?]
(A) *ú-du-ḫu* 319:8

Uzu-zari
(A) *ú-zu-za-ri* 322:i:6'

Waḫra-[xx] [H?]
(A) **wa-aḫ-ra*[*-x*] 244:ii:21'. From Rataman.

Wana-zu [H?]
(A) *wa-na-su* 244:ii:12'

Wanti-ya
(A) *wa-an-ti-ya* 224:30; 233:4 [SANGA ᵈIŠKUR].

ᶠWara-e
(C) *wa-ra-e* 207:i:21; 208:i:21. Palace servant.

Wurḫa-še
(A) *wu-úr-ḫa-ši* 322:iv:26

Zana-pan [H?]
(A) *za-⌜na⌝-ba-⌜an?⌝* 244:ii:20'

Zatu-ri [H?]
(A) *za-tu-ri* 318:12; 319:9. Heads a section. 320:ff (7 X).

Zazza-wiš [H?]
(C) *za-az-za-wi-iš* 267:4; 269:4; 270:4; 271:4. Receives beer.
za-al-za-wi-iš 268:4. An error rather than a variation of the name? Also receives beer.

Zigi (M)
(A) *zi-gi* 321:i:1

Zigi-ya
(A) *zi-gi-ya* 316:13. Receives barley.

Ziku-ya
(A) **zi-ku-ya* 244:ii:7'. From Rataman.

Zili-pan
(B) *zi-li-ba-an* Seal #11. Father of an important official.

ᶠZira-ḫu
(C) *zi-ra-ḫu* 207:i:12; 208:i:12. Palace servant.

ᶠZira-ri
(A) *ᶠ*zi-ra-ri* 225:10. From [Za]bri.

Zira-šše
(C) *zi-ra-áš-še* 188:6. Fisherman.

Ziri-tta
(A) *zi-ri-it-ta* 231:16. Cf. Mari's Ziri-tan.

Ziru [H?]
(A) *zi-ru* 236:7

Zizu-pa
(A) **zi-zu-pa?* 225:6. From [Za]bri.

Zu-ya
(A) *zu-ú-ya* 240:3

Zuzi-ya
(A) *zu-zi-ya* 224:36; 227:1, 4. Leader of a section.

Zuzu-[xx] [H?]
(A) **zu-zu-[xx]* 244:ii:25'. From Rataman

Zuzzi [- wari?]
(A) **zu-uz-zi* 232:11. From Marata. The name may be read, as below, *zu-uz-zi-wa?-ri*

Zuzzi-w[ari?]
(A) *zu-uz-zi-*P[I-ri] 224:1. Same name as above?

Zuzzu(n)-naya
(A) *zu-uz-zu-un-na-ya* 224:3

[xx]-kiriš
(B) [*x x*]-*ki-ri-iš* 6:rev:4'.

II,1. Unanalyzed Names

In this short list, I give names which have defied my ability to analyse within known linguistic groupings. For their occurrence in the Rimah archives, I refer the reader to the index of Personal Names given on pp. 257-264 of *The Old Babylonian Tablets from Tell al Rimah.*

a-ra/rá-(ar)-ra

a-ri-su-na(?)

ba-ri-na-ak

bu-uz-zi

⌈e-ge-en-na-ad-ḫi

e-wa-ra-ka-nu-um (cf. Ewar-kali, AAN, 47b)

ha-at-te/ti

ḫi-za-al(?)-lu

ḫu-zi-ri (cf. NPN, 66b; AAN,64b)

ḫu-zu-ku-uk

ku-du-li/lu-zi

mu-ra-ḫa-nu-ka

na-az-za-gu-ul-la

ni-ik-za-bi

nu-i-su-zi-na (cf. *nu-i-zi-qa*, AAN, 102a)

pár-ša-at-ta-ya

pa-(aš)-ši-it-ḫe 207:i:5; 208:i:5; 210:i:4 (not in index)

sa-an-ka

šu-bi-ḫi-x

ta-ap-ša-ḫi

ta-aš-mu-ya-x-x

te-et-ti-x	(cf. *te-et-ti*, AAN, 146a)
ti-gu	
za-ba-ar-da-x	
za-ḫa	
zi-in-nu-ga-nu	

III. List of Elements

This list of elements is patterned after the format presented in my study of Mari personal names. Numbers which follow the letters UF refer to those pages of the Mari article which either present or discuss the Hurrian elements at stake. New elements or variations to the elements listed in UF are given by reference to NPN (*Nuzi Personal Names* [OIP, 57] Chicago, 1943), Kilmer (A. E. Draffkorn [now A. D. Kilmer] *Hurrians and Hurrian at Alalah: An Ethno- Linguistic Analysis* [cited in note 2, above].

I should like to repeat the assertion, contained in UF, 375, "that citation [of elements] does not necessarily mean acceptance of interpretation offered [within these volumes]".

adal		UF 375a
	-adal	
		Alpu-adal
		Arum-adal
		Muzun-adal
		Nan-adal
		Nawar-adal
		Šaduk-adal
		Šaḫeš-adal
		^{d}U.GUR-adal
ag/k		UF 375a
	agap- [*aga+p*]	
		Agap-šeni
	aka-	
		Akata-tupki
	aku-	
		Aku-luk [H?]
al		
	alum- [*alu+m*]	
		^{f}Alu(m)-naya
alla(*i*)		UF 375a

allaš- [*alla+š*]
Allaš-arum

-allai
^{f}Alpuš-allai

alp NPN 199-200

alpu-
Alpu-adal
Alpu-ya

alpuš- [*alpu+š*]
^{f}Alpuš-allai

am(m)a UF 375b

aman [*ama+n*]
Aman-taḫi

an UF 375b

aniš [*ani+š*]
Aniš-kipal

-anu [uncertain, but the first part of the PN is likely to be Hurrian]
Šennip-anu [H?]

ar UF 375-376

aran- [*ara+n*]
Aran-[xx]

ari-
Ari-[xx]
Ari-ya(pa)

arip- [*ari+p*]
Arip-Teššub

arum- [*aru+m*]
Arum-adal
Arum-mušni

-arum [*aru+m*]
Allaš-arum

aranzi UF 376a (*sub* Aranziḫ)

-aranzi
Ḫazip-aranzi

at(t) UF 376b

atta(-)
Atta [H?]
Atta-ra [H?]

attap- [*atta+p*]
^{f}Attap-naya

aw		UF 376b
	awi-	
		Awi-yazu
		Awi-ziri
az(z)		UF 376b
	azip- [*azi*+*p*]	
		Azip-nan
	azzen [*az*(*z*)*i*+*n*]	
		^{f}Azzen
	azzu-	
		^{f}Azzu
		^{f}Azzu-e
		^{f}Azzu-ena
	-*azzu*	[not known elsewhere as second element]
		Kani-azzu
azni		[element?]
	-*azni*	
		Kanza-azni [H$^{?}$]
e		UF 376b
	-*e*	
		^{f}Azzu-e
		Šur-e
		Unuš-e [division uncertain; cf. Unu-še or Unuš-še]
		^{f}Wara-e
eḫl		UF 376-377
	eḫli-	
		Eḫli-a[xx]
		Eḫli-ya
el(*l*)		
	ella-	[cf. AAN, 43a]
		Ella-[xx] [H$^{?}$]
		Ella-li
	(-)*el*(*l*)*i*	
		Elli
		$^{(f)}$Unap-eli
en		UF 377a (*sub eni*)
	-*en*(*n*)*a*	
		^{f}Azzu-ena
		Ḫu-ena (or Ḫue-na)

		^{f}Tati-enna
er		NPN 210b
	era-	
		Era-ti [H?]
ewri		NPN 210-211 (sub *erwi*); Kilmer, 75 (sub *erwi*)
	-ewri	
		Talpunu-ewri [divide into Talpunu-wari or Talpu-nu—PI-ri]
		Teš(š)ub-ewri
ḫa		UF 377a
	-ḫam [*ḫa*+*m*]	
		^{f}Tizi-ḫam
ḫal		NPN 212-213
	ḫalu-	
		Ḫalu-li [H?]
ḫam		NPN 213a
	ḫamma-	
		Ḫamma-ta [H?]
ḫap		UF 377b
	ḫapi-	
		Ḫapi-ya [H?]
ḫaš		NPN 214; Kilmer, 76 (sub *ḫaž*)
	ḫaši-	
		Ḫaši-ya
ḫaz		UF 377b
	ḫazi-	
		Ḫazi-ya
	ḫazip- [*ḫazi*+*p*]	
		Ḫazip-aranzi
		Ḫazip-mu[xx]
		Ḫazip-Šimiga
ḫi		UF 377b
	-ḫi	
		Katir-ḫi
ḫirš/z		NPN 216a
	ḫirš/zi	
		Ḫirši-tta
		Ḫirzi-ya

ḫiu [unclear]

ḫiu-

Ḫiu-ya [H?]

ḫu NPN 217a

-ḫu

Utu-ḫu [H?]
[f]Zira-ḫu

ḫu(i/e) UF 377b; NPN 217 a (*sub ḫu*); 217b (*sub ḫui*)

ḫue-

Ḫue-na [or Ḫu-ena]

ḫul UF 377-378

-ḫul(i)

Šama-ḫul(i) [cf. Mari's Šam-ḫul]
Tallu-ḫul

ir(r)

irip- [*iri+p*]

Irip-zi [H?]

irri-

Itti-ki

itḫ NPN 221a; Kilmer, 81

itḫen [*itḫi/e+n*]

Itḫen-adal

itḫi-

Itḫi-ya

izz UF 378a

izza-

Izza-zzi

k

-k

Šaduk-adal

kka UF 378a-b

-kka

Kutu-kka
Nunna-kka
Tata-kka
Tiri-kka

kab/p UF 378b; Kilmer, 82

kap-

		Kap-tupki
	kaba-	
		Kaba-nnu [H?]
	kabi-	
		Kabi-nni
		Kabi-ya [cf. discussion in UF, 378b]
kadil [derivative of *kat* ?]		NPN 224a (*sub -katil*); 228b (*sub -kkatil*)
	-kadil	
		^{f}Nalu-kadil [H?]
kak(k)		NPN 222
	kak-	
		Kak-zu [H?]
	kakki-	
		Kakki-sĕ
	kakku- [?]	[Cf. sub *kan-* (?)]
		Kanaku-urši [H?]
kan(n)		UF 378b
	kan(n)a-	
		Kan(n)a-ya
		Kanaku-urši [H?]. Cf. sub *kakk-*, above.
	kani-	
		Kani-[xx]
		Kani-azzu
		Kani-ya
kanz		UF 379a; Kilmer, 83
	kanza-	
		Kanza-azni [H?]. Uncertain division.
		Kanza-ni
kaššil		Unattested elsewhere
	-kaššil	
		^{f}Menen-kaš^{s}<il [H?]
kat		NPN 224a (*sub katt*)
	-kate	
		Kenzu-kate [H?]
katir		UF 379a
	katir-	
		Katir-ḫi [H?]
ki		UF 379a

	-ki	
		Irri-ki
		[f]Puzum-ki
kib/p		UF 379b
	-kipal [*kipa*+*l*]	
		Aniš-kipal
ki/en(n)		UF 379a
	ken-	
		Ken-kiya/ziya
	kinni-	
		Kinni-ya [may well be W.S.]
kiya		NPN 224a (*sub-kiia*); 228b (*sub -kkeia*)
	-kiya	[read *ziya* ?]
		Ken-kiya/ziya
kinz/kenz		UF 379b. Cf. also *kizz*
	kinzi-	
		Kinzi-ya
	kenzu-	
		Kenzu-kate [H?]
kir		UF 379b
	-kiriš	
		[x x]-kiriš
kiz(z)		UF 379b
	kizzi	
		Kizzi
	kizzi-	
		Kizzi-pa [H?]
		Kizzi-pu [H?]
ku		NPN 228b
	-ku	
		Pazzi-ku [H?]
kui		NPN 228-229
	kui-	[Not known elsewhere in first position]
		Kui-tanu [H?]
kul(l)		NPN 229; cf. Kilmer, 85
	kullu	
		Kullu [H?]
	kul-	

		^{f}Kul-zipaya [division uncertain]
kun		UF 379b
	kun(u)-	
		Kun-tanu
		Kunu-zaḫi
kup		UF 379b
	kupa-	
		Kupa-ta [H?]
kut		UF 379b
	kuta-	
		^{f}Kuta-ti
	kuti-	
		Kuti-ya
	kutu-	
		Kutu-kka
kuz		UF 380a
	kuzi-	
		Kuzi-zu
l		UF 380a
	-l	
		Aniš-kipal
laya		*la+ya* (?) ; cf., NPN 231b (*sub -la*); 232a (*sub -lla*)
	-laya	
		^{f}Mennu-laya
		^{f}Tazu-laya
li		UF 380a
	-li	
		Ella-li
		Ḫalu-li [H?]
llu		NPN 232a
	-llu	
		^{f}Šila-llu [H?]
luk		UF 380a
	-luk	
		Aku-luk [H?]
m		UF 380a
	-m	
		Allaš-arum
		^{f}Tizi-ḫam

	-*m*(+ element)	
		^{f}Alu(m)-naya
		Arum-adal
		Arum-mušni
		^{f}Puzum-ki
		Šattum-ar[x]
		^{f}Šeḫlum-tari
ma		UF 380a
	-*ma*	
		Nuza-ma
men(*n*)		UF 380b
	menna	
		^{f}Menna
	menen-(*mene*+*n*)	
		$^{(f)}$Menen-kaššil [H?]
	mennu-	(does not occur with *u̥* in Nuzu or Alalaḫ)
		^{f}Mennu-laya
muz		UF 380b
	muzun- (*muzu*+*n*)	
		Muzun-adal
	-*mušni*	
		Arum-mušni
n		UF 381a
	-*n*(-)	
		Aran-[xx]
		^{f}Azzen
		Aman-taḫi
		$^{(f)}$Menen-kaššil [H?]
		Muzun-adal
		^{f}Šalan-zar
na		UF 381b
	-*na*	
		(Ḫue-na or Ḫu-ena)
		^{f}Ute-na [H?]
nadki		UF 381b
	-*nadki*	
		Šawalum-nadki
nal		Note possible element *nal*- in PNs such as Naltuya and Naltukka, assessed sub *nalt*, NPN 237b
	nalu-	

		^{f}Nalu-kadil [H$^{?}$]
nan		UF 381b
	nan-	
		Nan-adal
	-nan	
		Azip-nan
naw		NPN 238a (sub *nau*)
	nawa-	
		Nawa-nu [H$^{?}$]
nawar		UF 381b (related to *naw* ?)
	nawar-	
		Nawar-adal
naya		UF 381-382
	-naya	
		^{f}Alu(m)-naya ^{f}Attap-naya (Šešwe-[naya]) Zuzzu(n)-naya
n(n)i		UF382a
	-n(n)i	
		Kabi-nni Kanza-ni Ura-ni
n(n)u		NPN 240b
	-n(n)u	
		Kaba-nnu [H$^{?}$] Nawa-nu [H$^{?}$] Peza-nu [H$^{?}$]
nui		NPN 240b
	nui-	
		Nu-ya
nun		Unclear. Note Kilmer, 94 (sub *nuni-*)
	nunna-	
		Nunna-kka
	-nunu	
		Tampu-nunu [H$^{?}$]
nup		NPN 241a
	nupur-	(not attested elsewhere; but cf. Mari's Nupuri)

Nupur-šarri

*-nu-*PI*-ri* (For *nuri* ? cf., perhaps, NPN 241a *sub nur*)

*-nu-*PI*-ri*

Talpu-nu-PI-ri (or Talpunu-wari)

nuz UF 382

nuza-

Nuza-ma

pa UF 382b

-pa

Kizzi-pa [H?]
Zizu-pa

-pan (*pa+n*)

Zili-pan

pak UF 382b; NPN 242b

paki-

Paki-ya

pal UF 382b

pala-

Pala-tanu [H?]

pap NPN 243a

papa-

Papa-zzu [H?]

pap(p)i-

Pap(p)i-zu [H?]

paz(z) NPN 244a

pazzi-

Pazzi-ku [H?]

pez NPN 246a (*sub piz(z)*)

peza-

Peza-nu [H?]

pi UF 383a

-pi

Šuku-pi [H?]

pu NPN 246a

-pu

Kizzi-pu [H?]

puz Cf., NPN 248a, *sub* puza (?)

	puzum- (*puzu* + *m*)	
		[f]Puzum-ki
ri		UF 383b
	-*ri*	
		Zatu-ri [H?]
		[f]Zira-ri
š		UF 383b
	-*š*(+ element)	
		Allaš-arum (note that *a* before *š* is singular)
		[f]Alpuš-allai
		Aniš-kipal
		Šaḫeš-adal
šad/t		UF 384a
	šaduk- (*šadu* + *k*)	
		Šaduk-adal
	šattum-(*šattu* + *m*)	
		Šattum-ar[xx]
šaḫ		UF 384a
	šaḫeš- (*šaḫe* + *š*)	
		Šaḫeš-adal
šal		UF 384a
	šalan- (*šala* + *n*)	
	[f]Šalan-zar	
šam		UF 384a
	šama-	
		Šama-ḫul(i)
šarri		UF 384
	-*šarri*	
		Nupur-šarri
ša-PI-lum		UF 384b
	ša-PI-lum-	
		Šawalum-nadki
š(š)e		UF 384b
	-*š(š)e*	
		Kakki-še
		[f]Šeke-šše [H?]
		Unap-še
		Unu-še (or Unuš-(š)e/

		Unuš-e)
		Wurḫa-še
		Zira-šše
šeḫl		UF 384b
	šeḫlum- (*šeḫlu* + *m*)	
		^{I}Šeḫlum-tari
šek		NPN 254b (*sub šek*); 257a (*sub šikiia*)
	šeke-	
		^{I}Šeke-šše
	šikku-	
		Šikku-z(z)i
šešw		NPN 256b
	šešwe	
		Šešwe[-naya (?)]
šen(n)		UF 384-385
	šennip-	
		Šennip-anu [H?]
	-šeni	
		Agap-šeni
šil		NPN 254-255 (sub *šel(l)*)
	šila-	
		^{I}Šila-llu [H?]
šuk		UF 385a
	šuku-	
		Šuku-pi [H?]
Šimiga		NPN 257. Sun god
	-Šimiga	
		Ḫazip-Šimiga
šur		UF 385a
	šur-	
		Šur-e
ta		UF 385b
	-ta-	
		Akata-tupki
	-t(t)a	
		Ḫamma-ta [H?]
		Ḫirši-tta
		Kupa-ta [H?]

		Ziri-tta
taḫ		UF 385b
	taḫi	
		Taḫi
	-taḫi	
		Aman-taḫi
tak		UF 385b
	taki-	
		Taki-[xx]
		Taki-ya
tal(l)		NPN 262a; Kilmer, 107
	tallu-	
		Tallu-ḫul
talp		For *talm* ?; if so, see UF 386a
	talpu-	
		Talpu-nu-PI-ri or Talpunu-wari/ewri
tamp		For *tap(p)* ?; see UF 386a
	tampu-	
		Tampu-nunu [H$^{?}$]
tan		UF 386a
	-tanu	
		Kui-tanu [H$^{?}$]
		Kun-tanu
		Pala-tanu [H$^{?}$]
tar		Unattested elsewhere.
	-tari	
		^{f}Šeḫlum-tari
tat		NPN 263b
	tata-	
		Tata-kka
	tati-	
		^{f}Tati-enna
taz		NPN 264a
	tazu-	
		^{f}Tazu-laya
Teš(š)ub		Storm God; UF 386
	Teš(š)ub-	
		Teš(š)ub-ewri

	-Teššub	
		Arip-Teššub
ti		386a (*sub te*)
	-ti	
		Era-ti [H$^{?}$]
		^{f}Kuta-ti
tir		NPN 267b, *sub tiriku*
	tiri-	
		Tiri-kka
tiš/z		UF 386b
	tizi-	
		^{f}Tizi-ḫam
tuk		See below, sub *tupk*
tulp		NPN 268b
	tulpi-	
		Tulpi-ya
tupk/tukk		UF 386b
	tukki-	(cf. NPN 268b; Kilmer, 110)
		Tukki-[xx]
	tupki-	
		Tupki-[xx]
		Tupki-ya
	-tupki	
		Akata-tupki
		Kap-tupki
tutt		NPN 270; Kilmer 111
	tutta-	
		Tutta-ya [H$^{?}$]
^{d}U.GUR		UF 387a
	^{d}U.GUR-	
		^{d}U.GUR-adal
uk(k)		UF 387a
	uke	
		^{f}Uke
	ukka-	Ukka-[ya$^{?}$]
	uku-	
		Uku-nnu
un		UF 387

	unap-	
		(f)Unap-eli Unap-še
	unu(š)-	
		Unu-še or Unuš-e or Unuš-(š)e.
ur		UF 387b
	ura-	
		Ura-ni
urš		NPN 273b
	-urši	
		Kanaku-urši [H?]
ut		NPN 273-274; Kilmer. 113: "apparently not of H. origin, but common in H. onomastic usage."
	ute-	
		fUte-na [H?]
	utu-	
		fUtu-ḫu [H?]
uz		UF 387b
	uzu-	
		Uzu-zari
wa(=PI)-*ri*		Or *ewri*; UF 387b (*sub wari*); NPN 210-11 (*sub erwi*); Kilmer, 75 (*sub ewri*). See above *Nu*-PI-*ri*
	-PI-*ri*	
		Talpunu-wari or Talpu-nu-PI-ri
wan		NPN 274b
	wana-	
		Wana-zu [H?]
want		NPN 274b
	wanti-	
		Wanti-ya
war		UF 387b
	wara-	
		fWara-e
	wari-	cf. also sub *ewri*, *nu-PI-ri* Talpunu-wari)or Talpunu-ewri; Talpu-nu-PI-ri)
wiš		Unattested elsewhere.
	-wiš	
		Zazza-wiš (var. Zalza-wiš) [H?]

wurḫ		NPN 276a
	wurḫa-	
		Wurḫa-šė
ya		UF 387-388
	-ya	
		Alpu-ya
		Ari-ya
		Eḫli-ya
		Ḫapi-ya [H?]
		Ḫaši-ya
		Ḫazi-ya
		Ḫiu-ya [H?]
		Hirzi-ya
		Kabi-ya
		Kani-ya
		Kan(n)a-ya
		Kinzi-ya
		Kuti-ya
		Nu-ya
		Paki-ya
		Taki-ya
		Tulpi-ya
		Tupki-ya
		Tutta-ya [H?]
		Ukka-ya
		Wanti-ya
		Zigi-ya
		Ziku-ya
		Zu-ya
		Zuzi-ya
yaz		UF 388a
	-yazu	
		Awi-yazu
zaḫ		UF 388
	-zaḫi	
		Kunu-zaḫi
zar		UF 388b
	-zar	
		fŠalan-zar
	-zari	
		Uzu-zari
zat		UF 388b
	zatu-	
		Zatu-ri [H?]

zaz(z)		NPN 277a
	zazza-	(*zalza-* ?)
		Zazza-wiš (Żalza-wiš) [H?]
z(z)i		UF 388b
	-z(z)i	
		Irip-zi [H?]
		Izza-zzi
		Šikku-z(z)i
zik/g		UF 388b
	zigi(-)	
		Zigi
		Zigi-ya
	ziku-	
		Ziku-ya
zil		NPN 277-278
	zili-	
		Zili-pan
zipaya		NPN 278b
	-zipaya	
		^{f}Kul-zipaya
zir		UF 388b
	zira-	
		^{f}Zira-ḫu
		^{f}Zira-ri
		Zira-šše
	ziri-	
		Ziri-tta
	ziru	
		Ziru [H?]
	-ziri	
		Awi-ziri
ziz		UF 388-389
	zizu-	
		Zizu-pa
z(z)u		NPN 278-279
	zu-	
		Zu-ya
	-z(z)u	
		Kak-zu [H?]
		Kuzi-zu

Papa-zzu [H?]
Pap(p)i-zu [H?]
Wana-zu [H?]

zuz(z) UF 389b

zuz(z)i-

Zuzi-ya
Zuzzi [-wari?]
Zuzzi-w[ari?]

zuzzu-

Zuzu- [xx] [H?]
Zuzzu(n)-naya